Ishmael's Violets

Ishmael's Violets

Poems by

Vivian Eyre

© 2023 Vivian Eyre. All rights reserved.
This material may not be reproduced in any form, published,
reprinted, recorded, performed, broadcast,
rewritten or redistributed without
the explicit permission of Vivian Eyre.
All such actions are strictly prohibited by law.

Cover art "Intoxicating Scent of Salt" by Mary Dondero
Cover design by Sasha Wizansky
Author photo by Jen Lial

ISBN: 978-1-63980-463-4

Kelsay Books
502 South 1040 East, A-119
American Fork, Utah 84003
Kelsaybooks.com

Also by Vivian Eyre

To the Sound (chapbook)

For all species imperiled and vanished

Acknowledgments

With gratitude to the editors and journals where these poems first appeared, some under different titles, others in different forms:

Bard's Anthology: "Bucket to the Brim"
Book of Matches: "Catalog of Acceptances," "Photo of an Oyster Dredge"
Buddhist Poetry Journal: "Of Offerings"
Finishing Line Press: "The Fisherman's Daughter"
The Fourth River: "Whale Watch," "Like Bait"
J Journal: "Edit in Gasps of Wonder"
The Massachusetts Review: "The Circle of Several Centers"
Nine Mile: "Broken Free from Moorings"
One Art: "Summer Speaking in Turn"
The Orchards Poetry Journal: "Hearing Test"
Notable Works: Voices of the Earth: "Morning of the Great Whale Spirit"
Pangyrus: "Afterlife"
The Sandy River Review: "Fudgie the Whale," "Aquarium"
The Santa Ana Review: "The End"
Spire: "Ode to the Cold-Stunned Sea Turtle," "What the Sea Told Me"
SWWIM: "Widening Rings"
Turtle Island Quarterly: "The Whale House," "Speak, Memory"
Twelve Mile Journal: "Names That Separate"

With deep gratitude to Terese Svoboda and Juliet Patterson who believed in the manuscript from the beginning; to Kara Hoblin and Cindy Pease Roe for the first sparks of inspiration; to Cynthia Bargar and Wendy Drexler with deep gratitude for generous and insightful critique at a critical juncture; to Miranda Beeson and Elizabeth Sylvia with special appreciation for astute commentary; to my dear weekly writing group: Cynthia Bargar, Wendy Drexler,

Xiaoly Li, Steve Nickman, Sarah Dickenson Snyder, Connemara Wadsworth, Margot Wizansky my heartfelt thanks for feedback and friendship; to my accomplished poets and friends: Jane Bachner, Anna Birch, Heidi Dube, John Heavey, Shana Hill, Alexis Ivy, Lin Illingworth, Phyllis Katz, Duffy Kopriva, Linda Megathlin, Myrna Patterson, Susan Pizzolato, Marilyn Potter, Carol Sabia, Elizabeth Sylvia, LB Thompson, Carolyn Windham with gratitude for ongoing support and sharing the journey; to Mary Dondero, Jen Lial and Sasha Wizansky with tremendous thanks for your artistry; to the Brunch Poem discussion group at Floyd Memorial Library my abiding gratitude; to baseball; to Kelsay Books for selecting this manuscript; to The Center for Coastal Studies and New York Marine Rescue Center with profound gratitude for saving the lives of whales and sea turtles; to New Bedford Whaling Museum, Southold Historical Museum and Imago Foundation for the Arts my sincere thanks; to Tina Cane, Kimiko Hahn, Brenda Hillman, Matthew Olzmann, William Packard, Carl Phillips, Paul Nicklen, Dan Beachy-Quick, Tracy K. Smith with utmost gratitude for your work and what you've taught me; to my sister, Donna Vannata and Carylyn Waite with deep love; and to my father, of course.

Contents

What the Sea Told Me	15
When Whales Walked	19
Whale Shot	20
The Circle of Several Centers	21
Whale Watch	23
Edit in Gasps of Wonder	24
Provincetown Lobster Diver Swallowed by a Humpback Whale on Jimmy Kimmel Live	25
Considering the Price of a Lobster Roll	26
Ishmael's Hands	28
DAY BOOK	31
My Middle Is Misery	43
The End	44
Speech Bubble	45
To Fudgie the Whale	46
Hearing Test	47
Letter to Rachel Carson	48
Names That Separate	50
After Reading the Scrimshaw Dictionary I Write Some Letters	52
Like Bait	57
Speak, Memory	59
Our Lady of the Seas Nursing Home	60
Missing	61
Ode to the Cold-Stunned Sea Turtle	62
The Visible Invisibility of Danger	63
Catalog of Acceptances	64
Aquarium	65
The Fisherman's Daughter	66
Photograph of an Oyster Dredge Greenport Harbor (circa 1940)	67
Bucket to the Brim	68
Floods	69

Broken Free from Moorings	70
Morning of The Great Whale Spirit	71
Theft	72
Summer, Speaking in Turn	75
Ode to the Sea Turtle Rescuers	76
Of Offerings	77
Power Naps	78
Scrolling Backward	79
Afterlife	80
Widening Rings	81
The Whale House	82

What the Sea Told Me

Lately I've been practicing to stay.
I stand here like a sea wall.
It's too cold to sit down. At the water's edge
scoured by rollers, there's a glacial moraine
flat-topped like a seat. Maybe it's a chair rock
where the ancients once sat with their guides
at sunrise asking for the sea's blessing.
In this kingdom of slate-gray waves,
I have slipped far down into myself.
On cobbles of feldspar and quartz
my fears rise. If only I had paws
or a leaning staff to walk across
what doesn't give. A rush of wind
through my coat, that urge to turn away,
that old way to flee. It came to me
like a person: What changes me
is outside of me. The riprap loosens.
A kind of grace how I found this cove.
Without the asphalt road cutting through
the corridor of pines, lofty shadows,
      juncos & sparrows,
without the villager's hand-sketched map,
I never would have heard the sea's words—
Come closer.

I.
Melville tried to warn us. The world is an elusive whale:
we might choose coexistence or destruction.
And though we do not decide the outcome,
the hands on the oars are ours;
each stroke invites consequences.

—Carl Safina

When Whales Walked

And they first walked on land four-legged,
dog-sized, with a sudden canter of hooves
      from a lineage of horses, pigs, hippos
      becoming part of the tropical jungle
of everything, part of the earth
of swamp cypress, big-eyed turtles,
      enormous Ibis, flightless ducks,
      part of the wet swelter and sweat,
of both sides of killing, part of divinity,
of the land with no handprints, of nothing
      to buy, part of ever-shifting time,
      goodbye to land time; to survive.
The answer to why whales entered the sea's doorway
is silence. Sure, the few grasses grew fewer
      and tiny *Knightia* gorged in rivers and lakes
      where the whales fed and tails widened
as feet thickened to paddles,
as ear bones swallowed each underwater swish,
      and the hind limbs drew into the body
      the way landing gear retracts, invisible,
but still there. How their babies' eager glia let foremothers
      slip away, shedding fur for mythic skin.

Whale Shot

Livestream on Instagram

Seated in a shallow craft, the red-bikini girl.
Expanse of ocean, a blue-gray backdrop.
With eyes flashing light, her lithe body
swivels to smile at the camera lens.
A long thick shadow sidles up.
The voice behind the lens says:
Oh my god. Turn around. Look.
I see it. The orca's head rising,
slick from the sea mouth.
Over mystery's rim, sheening
with suntan oil, her fingers skim
the whale's thin, translucent skin—
know nothing of how the oxides
soak through. This one touch
lifts the girl weightless
from the gravity of her land-body.
Yes, I too, have touched wonder,
washed my hands without washing
the one I touched.

The Circle of Several Centers

It was all visible at the water's surface—
how the mother orca swam pushing her calf

in front or carried its body on her forehead's swelling,
or in her mouth—which meant she couldn't eat.

Was she trying to rouse, spark, kick-start
the lungs, the way hope can be part reflex?

The mist of thirty blowholes behind the mother wake,
each whale taking a turn to push.

How wide is the circumference of loss?

Whether the sky was moonlit or moonless
and by the sun's travel lamp,

she swam pushing/carrying her calf,
one hundred miles in a circle. Twice.

It takes time to loosen the twists
in a figure eight knot.

But how to square the heartbeats,
briefly there,

like tiny kicks

inside a mother's belly
as that mother folds
the never-used onesie

into a plastic bag.

How big must a brain be
to feel sadness—mouth-feel of salt,

swimming so close to loss, the closeness
so visible above the water's surface.

Whale Watch

after Kara Hoblin's watercolor, Whale

Whale, the color of moonlight,
so pale that I see inside the body,
the bones sketched in lamp black ink.
The enveloping seas like bruises:
aubergine, pink, hospital green.
I want my arms around this body.
The long streamlined knobby spine
I long to touch before
she breaches out of the sea,
twirls acrobatically mid-air,
plunges with one brash slap to break open
the sea door. I want to caress the flesh,
ripped at the flare of the fluke
by iron barbs or blunt force blows.
I want the flipper, the bony flanges,
so like a human hand, in my hands,
as light as a scrim of mist.

Edit in Gasps of Wonder

Although the channel was off limits,
he was steering there. For the tip jar to fill,
they had to see whales. The baby whale backflipped
away from its mother. From the sundeck, this was clear.
That single breath geysered too close to the boat.

      Like this—he'd said later, after a gulp of Bud,
rocking his hands side to side—how the boat shook
when the whale and its mother swam under the hull.
Like a mini-van and double wide bus.
It took time to cut the engines, he'd said.

Sitting next to him at the dive bar,
I could picture those white-pleated torpedoes.
That velvet rushing toward four-blade propellers.
It was useless to ask if the whales' skin
had been scraped or gashed. He was swallowed
by the *oh/oh/oh* from a coterie of tank tops,
buying rounds to salute that onboard day.
I heard him say: *Who will cruise with me tomorrow?*

Provincetown Lobster Diver Swallowed by
a Humpback Whale on Jimmy Kimmel Live

I wasn't technically swallowed, the diver says.
Jimmy says, I got a show to do; I'm going with swallowed.

Inside the wide-open mouth of a paper mâché whale, that diver
sits, knees bent, like a boy scrunched into a bumper car.

Eyes shuttering, he recalls the sensation as if inside a car hurtling
headlong into the churn of sea, whiplash raising his neck hair.

Under stage lanterns, his face reddens. The blush of death
flushed out in front of a live audience. They laugh, teeth showing,

like the laughter of Romans when lions rushed into the Colosseum.
The songs of our indifference. From the farthest distance, I

can glide into the diver's fears. My first terror, the dive,
gulped into the sea's pit. My arms feeling paper-thin.

And dear whale—what did you feel when that force crossed
your home's threshold and entered you? I know it's not right

to imagine you feel like me. But you do use language, after all.
Something was wounded when that diver kicked you

until you spit him out. My tongue touches scar tissue, the knotted
line inside my cheek. My body is an archive with spectacles,

emptiness, with resurrections returning us to the abyss,
to the gulf of communion wider than a giant mouth agape.

Considering the Price of a Lobster Roll

In Wellfleet, we stop at that family-owned fish shack.
These sweeties come at a price, $28 apiece.

So, we split one roll: jam-packed with tail flesh, chunked, cold,
blushed in mayo on a grilled buttered bun. What doesn't register

is this sandwich costs more than the polypropylene rope
knotting the buoy to the trap, less than the trap,

less than the life of any right whale swimming through the ocean,
mouth open as she must, gasps of glittery krill. Among seaweed,

the biting tongues of jellyfish, the vertical rope is camouflaged.
The rope entangles the whale's head, fins—saws into her jaw.

She doesn't know there's no wiggling from the wraps.
She knows how to thrash her fluke fiercely until blood blooms

in the boils of white water. We cut the lobster roll in half
with a plastic knife which doesn't saw unless you bear down.

Right whale babies also shrouded in rope.
Without Houdini's magic. Entanglements

named *Whaling by Mistake*. Some say, Really?
Some say, I have a right to make a living.

While the count of North Atlantic right whales shrink
(500, 425, 349), everyone takes sides.

Our orders come without sides of cole slaw and fries.
This mistake is easily fixed. While eating

my lobster roll, I talk about my father's love of lobster in a bath
of drawn butter. The plastic bib always arrived too late.

Across his shirt, I could see those tiny traps of lipids
lining his heart's byways. My father asked for the Last Rites,

although he didn't believe. I pray for the last rights, not
knowing where those pleas will land.

Ishmael's Hands

Ishmael smelled violets while standing
inside the mansion of a whale head,
when the oil was warmest, easiest to bucket
right after slicing off the whale crown.

The violet incense drifted Ishmael into
the sanctum sanctorum of whale.
Steeped in a dream, his hands pumped
globes of fat that broke

into opulence. In a frenzy of grasping
beneath the pool, Ishmael squeezed the hand
of a mate or phantom or a divine hand.
He didn't care.

He was held by what he couldn't hold.
Of course, this is all fiction.
Of course, the truth is too large
for one point of view. Ishmael

never stood in a meadow of spring violets—
only a meadow of unhinging,
tongue-tied with bliss, forgetting
how easy it is to slip

off a keeling ship or into
the oily pool of head gold.

II.
If you find any sand in this letter,
regard it as so many sands of my life,
which run out as I was writing it.

—Herman Melville

DAY BOOK

Journal poems after beach walks

~

Along the backbone of this island, the sand
combines with silt, gritty debris left behind
by moving glaciers. The remains amass
forming boulders, their cold children.
The sea greets me without asking.
It must be the rhythm of her gray waves
that deepens my breath, untangles
my bandaged days. My hand
finally free from the cast's binding.
I begin to ditch what rains inside me
when my water shoe hits something tinny.

Found

a souvenir of our country
left behind in a footprint's swale.
This shiny metal can.
No longer the *King*. No *Weiser.*
Stamped with a newly scripted *A—*
America is in your hands.

~

Beach blankets like rows of stamps.
I think about Dickinson who never saw the sea,
but visioned the tide chasing a child—I sight
a swarm of dark flutters like winged Harpies
landing slapdash among the eel grass.

She has some ghostly Fright come up
And stop to look at her

Waving at me, the surrender flags of our cravings:
golden, cheddar, sweet chili, sour cream,
polypropylene bags, hieroglyphs, grammar
of our freedoms. Our yearnings ditched
within the grasp of the sea's outstretched hands.

Found

Praise, the brigade marching with brown trash bags
stuffed into back pockets like plastic tail feathers
of futuristic birds. They capture stray oddments:
cheese wrappers, trails of oranges, shiny bits,
liquor nips. If they grow hungry, bored, feel faint
under blisters of sun, no one's the wiser.

~

At the shoreline, a girl steps into an inflated green seahorse,
long snout, jagged mane. Into the lacy water, she trots,
flutter-kicks into delight. Waves crest over the rim
of rubber, mysterious how the color changes green to blue—
the way real seahorses do. Their promenade and pirouette.
Don't go too far, her mother calls out. That voice
I hear behind me/inside me. A girl's enchantments
glitter onto the waves, lost, swept away to an island.

Years later she finds those delights while beachcombing
mica, iridescent jingle shells, Venus combs.

Found

A pile of blunts, burnt matches,
sea-washed pack of Camels.

A father puts out his cigarette on sand,
so he can smooth the wheat-colored hair
of his sleeping child. If I asked the father
why, would he say: What litter?
What if harm is the conductor and we,
the perpetual band, are the fiddlers?

~

As we step over swags of matted seaweed,
black flies swarm up. My friend says
she's learned how to embody joy while standing
in a certain ballet position. Tangleweed, she says
her life is, a need to shed. The word *SHED*
dangles in front of me like a magician's patter
and switch. I slip out of my body. Transported
by meddlesome seaweed sloughing off rocks,
choking boat motors, tugging at the articulation of
bathers' legs. The clouds break apart when her light touch
grazes my arm—*Let me show you again how to breathe.*

Found

A brittle star.
Four spiny arms,
twist and coil
around sea lace fronds.
One arm missing.

~

I've let beaches loosen my tongue, uncover words
unutterable in cafes or bedrooms. That couple
lying on sand, fully clothed. He's propped up
on his elbow, words rippling out. The quiet
of his looking down. Whatever is said, rift
or union, furrows between the grains of sand,
remains, forgotten there. Their bodies lean in,
her hand to his cheek—the way I've touched
a child's cheek who told me the sea has a secret
pocket filled with our dreams.

Found

Scavengers divebomb the beach
with blue & white bottle caps.
Some lids land in the sand bed
where that couple lay. Some
on a clutch of broken clam shells.
The beach must be exhausted from
a lifetime of acceptance: our comings,
our goings, every leave behind.

~

On sand, a floor plan of rooms
outlined in stones, hand-sized stones,
pitted, mottled, stones from earth's oven.
I enter where stones separate. In one room,
a driftwood log as long as a telephone pole
likely homed here by storms teeming
with tide. Inside the circle of burnt coals,
I find charred bamboo sticks, one with
a crisped marshmallow, half-eaten.

Some someones chose to come here.
Not to a parking lot, mall, tree house or cave.
This dwelling, this place to remain, remaining
part of the sea, their impermanent home,
home to be inhabited by.

Found

Who sees the sea's erasure?

With a driftwood stick, I write
in wet sand: *I Was Here*
I Was
I

~

At the strand, four fishermen line up.
Windbreakers billow, convoy of blue sails.

Lines cast off. Tugs in drifting tide,
the reeling in. No one catches the wished-for.
No one loses bait. They blame wind, heat,
lures, passing motorboats. The silent buckets.

Found

A boy throws stones into the surf. *Fai presto!*
Hurry up, Paolo, the old man calls then
turns to me: *I knew last night no fish but the boy*
wanted to try. He shrugs the shrug of helpless love.
Last night seals sashayed around a nearby harbor.
The water's touch tells the fish, the man says,
his arm circling the boy's shoulders. I smile,
having known the grands' harbor of arms.
I know birds follow fish. Today a bird-less sky.

~

What are you looking for?
Anything.

Up to his ankles in bay, minnows swim
beyond his red fishing net. Glimmering silver
moors the boy so utterly. His net stabs water,
widening the gaps in knotted string.
Anything isn't found.
What remains behind the sandcastle
doused in light—a blue plastic shovel.
Sand can be a keeper.
Anything can be found easily in sand.

Found

Where the berm ends and the surf collide,
below a tall nesting platform,
this toppled nest exposing its innards.
Between twigs and muddy reeds,
a blue plastic shovel entwined with mistakenness:
plastic bags pass for sea lettuce, a stutter of
crimped balloon ribbons doubles as pale eel grass.
What worries me is the sharp-eyed osprey,
blind to what tangles foot-leg-wing.

~

Sometimes I sit here watching the waves swell, surge,
blend into each other like memories, this fear
like plastic stockpiles on the island of debris. I'm afraid
to swim because my arm is a shipwreck that cannot be raised.
Sometimes the light casts a kind of mercy on the dutiful,
furious waves, over these seas of indifference,
over our fragile earthliness.

III.
A child crying gives away his hiding place,
but a silent child is forgotten.

—Yehuda Amichai

My Middle Is Misery

You don't want to forget you're human. You sizzle, blaze
as if at an Elvis concert. On the screen,

another sheened mama's boy, the orca Tilikum
torpedoes up from a shallow pool to fetch a frisbee.

Dances the macarena on its muscled tail. Explosive forces
propel its body into the air as if hoisting a two-story house.

You're watching *Blackfish* caught in a swirl of superlatives,
in every *est* and *most*. Wet-slicked skin, tight

as the leather get-up Elvis wore for his comeback tour,
eyes glowering under the dangle of gelled bangs,

side smile of a menace, dangerous pelvis, the part animal
in all of us. Not that you threw your undies on stage.

But still. Beauty holds violence even in our ease. The white
jumpsuit, fringed, raised limbs look like wings, god-like

except for the sheets of sweat rolling down his swollen face.
Same pills handlers fed the orca, belly up on the pool deck.

Look what happens when you place a wild dream
in a cement tank and hand feed it. The hands are milking

the orca's long, engorged phallus for booty juice.
Come here, babies, says the factory of collusion, the eager,

the unwilling caught in misery's net. Inside of you,
where no one sees, you try to douse the flames,

for what we raise up we pull down. Look
at the night sky. It's moonless or else it's full of stars.

The End

*RIP the 175 orcas who have died
in captivity at marine parks.*

No one knows what plays in the mind's dark theater,
when ropes hold them afloat at the end.
What song-worm hums
a motionless whale body: mating trills,
eager tenor of takeaway ships,
or mother's cries because mothers cry
like animals for young ones lost. No one knows
what taste lingers in the mouth's recall: herring
or blood ribboning through
the red knotted thread—*Don't remember me,
but ah! Remember my fate.*
At the end, the flukes reflex to furl, unfurl
the last swim. Then through the portal,
a dream, a shimmering that follows mother's
deepest dive, beyond spout-smoke rising
beneath the ink-spilled moon.
Blackfish.

Speech Bubble

Under a beach umbrella, you flip
to the first *New Yorker* cartoon—
a whale beached on a sandflat.
The speech bubble's tail
points to the whale—
Next time I'll bring a book.
In your black Speedo,
your speech bubble says: *Hey,
that's me.* You're part universe
with sad eyes, bookless, dying gradually
miles away from your family. What
last book would this whale choose?
Certainly not Melville. You notice
the bottom corner: a plover.
Small, stocky, head lowered, searching
for worms in sand. Turning away
from the whale's last request.
It's not funny to make you think about
a bird's disinterest, beached whales,
your fragile connections, being human.
Those insistent bell ringers,
that damn Good Humor ice cream truck.

To Fudgie the Whale

When I saw you through that cellophane window
of the Carvel box, my shadow vanished into your deep

fudge glaze. I never heard of a whale-shaped ice cream cake,
or ice cream cake that wasn't iceberg dense.

When I spooned through the light vanilla
and chocolate layers, a soft *mmm* hummed inside me.

I'm not a fan of rubble in ice cream. But I forgave
the cookie crunchies, the edge of frosted rosettes,

not whale-ish at all. Fudgie. An icon
who lived in the boroughs. Cameos on Letterman,

and in-between innings at Shea. Hooray for Tom Carvel
whose favorite book was Moby Dick. He fathered you

on Father's Day. He piped a blue line of icing across your side—
For a Whale of a Dad. For all dads could be whale-kin

with the largest hearts and smarts and warm-blooded bonds.
Hooray for my dad, bringing you, Fudgie, to his BBQ.

Because in Brooklyn, goddesses were not sustained
by burnt offerings alone. Hooray for us, our thrills

when passing around the chipped plates,
as we pushed our folding chairs closer.

Hearing Test

Hearing aids on eBay—twenty dollars apiece
for a whale's inner ear bone (previously owned).

Its center hole is no bigger than a mouth
saying: *oh no.*

My fading ear no longer hears what it's offered—
like a muffled love song

beneath the drone of a vacuum. *What?*

Near Boston Harbor, right whales stop
blip/click talking

because hearing thins below
uba, moop, boom, nizz, the zither

vibes from biologists' hydrophones,
the throb of ships with liquid fire and fire rock.

Ships of ear plugs, voice buds, air pods, circuit boards.
Ships of wings. Ships of wheels, the rev & ro-ro.

Ships of wanderers, seekers, seers.
Whales give-up parsing noise,

finding a meal or love. Someone proposes:
Whales must learn to sing louder.

If the mind hears with its own ear harp,
can we hear the cry of the sea?

*A child crying gives away his hiding place,
but a silent child is forgotten.*

Glassed-in the museum's case, the quiet
harpoons, the blue footnotes of deftness.

Letter to Rachel Carson

1

Dear Rachel, It's Earth Day, the day you sparked. Forests thick on T-shirts. Copse of verdant hands raises a planet of trees planted on *Go Green* signs. Nothing of how life began as a watery globe, light nourishing sea shallows, deep shadows of refuge countering the wild swings of heat. Are we mapped to see the partial, to parse Mother from Nature? I have a motherload of questions to mull, I tell my friend. Does Rachel have a podcast? she asks.

2

I open *The Sea Around Us* to that dog-eared page. To that quiet colony of piping plovers, I say the words you wanted read at your candlelit burial rites: *Now I hear the sea sounds about me; the night high tide is rising, swirling with a confused rush—* your last wish, your friend promised to recite—but he didn't. *Silent Spring* was read instead. Not that I'm against debugging bug spray, deleting red Xs eaten by fish (and us), erasing toxic run-off. Silence can be scathing, tasteless, odorless, crystalline. It's monumental to blow out the candle of the sea
speaking in your tongue.

3

It's not that you wanted to see the Redwood Forest or wear diamonds or wanted your breasts back. You wanted time to write, to hear that sonic rush of wonder. I think about last wishes, my sister holding my hand, weight and warmth sealing three *I love yous* like hot wax on a letter. I've not made her promise, because of the miles between us and what can't be depended upon, because of the rift a last wish can make.

4

At the Woods Hole dock, I visit your bronze statue. You look like a teacher in that A-line skirt, legs crossed, circle pin circling the top button of your blouse. See how the lab coats wanted you in a pocket. That photo of you on a nature walk with children, bending down to talk as if you were their mother. You, who never had children. You, who predicted the seas rising while we watched *Father Knows Best*. I think about the long rhythms of your life, tempest and tide, how the young with dollars for gum have more muscle than your last wish.

5

If we can separate the forests from the sea, how easily we can disconnect from each other, cleave promises from friendship, screen off the vanished, the vanishing. Rachel, aren't our lives like water with their rushes, separations of sludge and settlings, their whirls and freezes? I wish I could talk with you about omission as a kind of diminishment. Splitting land from sea seems like the original hands ripping bone from flesh.

Names That Separate

after the whaling ship model named
after the shipbuilder, Morgan

1

On the side of the model, the cutting stage, a plank hung
so as not to slip off while flensing strips of blubber.

The try out pots, kettles where fat was boiled on the deck,
to "try out" oil's richness, rising stench and steam.

No name given to the whaleman
who named the whale

right,

who termed the slow surface skimmer
with curious eyes so close to the ship

right
the right whale to kill.

Never before had a whale been named
right. It felt right.

2

The names of the ship's crew written in a worn log:
John, the one God showed his favor upon.
Thomas, whose hand touched the sacred wound.
William, determined protector.

Christian names, entangled with the mayhem of being,
of whalers, of an enterprise plaited with belief:
the ocean would not fail. The whole venture,
not named: bloodbath, massacre, butchering, carnage,

branded candles, soap, margarine, transmission fluid, trench-
foot treatment, corset stays, parasols, shoehorns, hairbrushes,
eyeglass frames, hat rims, sofa stuffing, police night sticks,
canes—*to whale on*—those misbehaving school children.

After Reading the Scrimshaw Dictionary
I Write Some Letters

~

Letter to Joseph Bogart Hershey,
the Young Whaleman

You felt it, the retreat, the way skin falls back
from a wound, how art is the lightest foothold
on the natural self, sealing off night tremors.
You invented the word *flowering* for landscapes,
flowerpots, balloons sketched on hollowed-out teeth,
softer in the mouth than *scrimshanding* with a *hand*
reaching for ruin. The needle scoring ivory
was the needle used to mend sails. Harder to stitch
in the shadows of waiting, your *mind deep pressed.*
You don't write the words *whale* or *slaughter,* only
a stock full of oil is cure for spirits dejected.
Does a precarious life wax sadness into violence?
You must have thought about whales all the time,
the stench of the animal could travel for miles.
You'd be surprised how little we think
about whales now. Although the same question surges
through the labyrinth: How much of life depends
upon art, upon ruin?

~

Letter to Sereno Edward Bishop,
the 12-year-old Cabin Passenger
on a Whaling Schooner

Were you a little night bird flying into the fire
on the schooner's deck? Were you like moonlight
that strobed the lonely faces of whalemen,
as you traveled alone to an unknown divinity
school? You have to love a thing to study it.
More closely than the sea birds circling the deck,
you studied the men who *caught three albatrosses
yesterday, although it was Sunday. They cannot fly
after they are on deck or walk it's ridiculous,*
the cruel mesh of the foot, the missing hind toe,
the wobble to stand up, wings seesawing, the birds
falling over. They *killed and skinned* them, you wrote,
but didn't say how or why. You must have stood
on the deck, your soles bloodied from bird and whale.
Did a frayed invisible light shield you
from the *I don't care* ways, from the wheel of day?
You must have carried those shiny parables
inside your chest, a nest of ashes.

IV.
Everything we see hides another thing.

—Claude Magritte

Like Bait

There's no turning away
from that x-ray
at the turtle rescue hospital.

~

It comes back to me,
the sweetness of fishing
alongside my sister. Sun
not yet reaching its zenith,
lines plunged into the dark border
under dock planks. The yank,
reel up, the hook cleanly cut
from the fishing line. My sister pointing,
Look, as a turtle popped up its head.
The thief, we laughed.
We guessed that turtle was a lucky sign
of fish schooling below. Again,
we baited the hook.

~

The hook.
The turtle swallowed
the wire, arched and tipped with a barb
biting into the pectoral lobe. The film's x-ray
blazing between the breastplates—a black dot,
a clot, the heart. I don't know whether
this was our "lucky turtle." Or not.

~

The first breast-plate armor worn
by the Great Turtle was a delicate seashell,
and the soil piled on its back grew into
the world. The legend goes.

~

Now in front of this turtle's x-ray, I see
what cannot be swallowed.

Speak, Memory

What do you think? My dad asks the shop boy
in the marine supply store. *They look great,* the teen nods

toward my dad's boat feet. I guess they did—considering
the cracks across the orthopedic sneakers

he had been wearing. *Plimsolls!* Dad announces, remarkably,
since he often calls me by my sister's name.

Later he'll ask the name of these boat shoes. *Sounds like . . .*
a gin cocktail, umbrella, pimples, the pine-scented aerosol.

Once I say, *Plimsoll,* he'll say: *load line
on a hull* as if we were playing the game: What is it?

It's the waterline on the hull of the ship
if the sea rises above the line, cargo drenches.

Here in this shop, Dad's stare, hypnotic, in the full-length mirror.
Staring at what? His tonsured head, the half-moon pouches

under his eyes, belly swell against the buckle's despair,
the patch where the needles for dialysis bit.

Okay son, he says. Not to the shop boy who's vanished.
Not to me. I want to believe that he's speaking to

the part of himself before nautical twilight—the stars
still bright enough to vessel out to sea.

Our Lady of the Seas Nursing Home

Never mind that Ida owns a bait shop
or her crew neck sweat is lettered *Surfs Up,*
mocking the prongs of her cannula tube.
Now she's waving at me in the stern of this room.
I'm temporarily beached here, she says
temporarily meaning a cozy blanket hiding the truth
meaning *when can I go home?*
meaning if only I could shamble along the shore
without sandbags tied to my breath entranced
by ospreys winging through swollen air meaning
how to hold this barely bearable hunger.
I hand her the white bakery bag, the sugar donuts
we both love, *mia cara amica.*
Ida's powdery fingers point to the tidal app,
her productive loneliness, where she tracks
rainfalls' gush, the winds' gut-shove,
the crowns of tides—even as the tides of her body rise.

Missing

to "Granny," the 100-year-old orca

Half-moon notched on your dorsal fin—
where did you swim that day
ahead of the pod? It seems unfathomable.
They lost you after listening so long
to your claps, clicks, scuttle & wobble.
Your last song. Your song
touched hydrophones listening to your mother tongue,
the glass sponge reefs, moon jellies, the silken
obsidian sleeve of the water column. Whalefall
like falling rain on soft sand, two worlds
elide into the last seconds of your breath
in the fathoms. No one can tell me how
your pod knew not to follow
the boat of your body
now yours
alone.

Ode to the Cold-Stunned Sea Turtle

Where in these nets of light, this tide
can I find you?

Once you knew how to nose out of the birth-egg's
shell with moonlight and stars, your signs,
to shimmy the downslope into open blue,

your body, all wobble. Your flippers quick-
slapped the undersea, a frantic rush
to cross the salty vastness. All your senses

trusting the way it's always been. How soundly
you slept in that blind-stitched sea pocket.
Missed the cue: the water's slow cooling. Yes,

the sea changes around us—
changes us—in ways we barely detect.

I hope this isn't true:

the only way I see
how much the sea has changed
is by losing you.

The Visible Invisibility of Danger

for T. Harte

Why did you hide it, I asked him, about the hawksbill tortoise
shell, the gutted beauty shell, left behind on a windowsill
by a former tenant in this Turtle Bay rental. Imperiled treasure,
novelty for pleasure receptor release. He said it made him shiver
to ride his motorbike, the Beauty, over the bridge. Wind with
more muscle than the power he rode. Danger's lingo, its own
loose-nets, nested in the woo, wild, unblinkered, his blue eyes
air-kissed. In the uncovered lot, his bike parked under a dark cape.
I hid it because your face blurred when you saw it he said or said
we can hear heartbreak tick inside silent hours without seeing it.
After he died, I found the shell of golden flecks entombed
in folds of his Donegal sweater. I touched each buffed serrated cut
on the turtle's under-shell. The rotary dial rang its bell, cued
his voice machine, his voice: Hello. You know what to do.

Catalog of Acceptances

Hart's Cove, Center Moriches Bay, L.I., NY.
November 15–21, 2016

Accept that curious bunker fish, thick & glittery,
    swarmed in the shallows.

Accept that the whale's hanker & the sandbar lay
    too close together.

Accept that the tide's six cycles of lows/highs are too weak
    to thrust the whale 30 feet into the ocean's channel.

Accept that the whale heart, its rhythmic pulse, is crushed
    by its weight. Sand-bar pinned.

Accept that sun's cauldron boils over isinglass skin.
    The gulls. The gulls.

Accept that the whale's song box folded/unfolded into a long wail
    shuddering through windows to the sleepless village.

Accept that the locals named the whale *Morey*.
    They called out: *Lord, for an ear and a dig-away.*

Accept that experts are hooked on mysteries.
    The whale's body had a story to tell.

Accept that a beach becomes a room of latex gloves, vials,
    the rongeur to gouge out bones, knives for sectioning.

Accept that the tow strap fastened the rags of carcass
    onto the truck slab.

Accept that locals played bagpipes at the end of Inlet Road
    and hammered into the yellow Dead-End sign

    a driftwood-carved black whale.

Aquarium

Feed the stingrays—
fingerprints smear the plexiglass sign.
Deep set eyes, wing-fins, wand-like
tails swirl and heave water over
the shallow pool rim. From a paper cup,
a girl flings a dried worm, like offerings
to cast spells of enchantment. The dried bit
drops to the blue rutted pool bottom
between the crevices. They find it.
Now it's your turn, the girl turns to me
with the air of maternal prowess. I kneel
to slow what I want/don't want to do next.
My hand plunges into the pool, so quick
a dark snout opens into a mouth slit,
satiny skin, an almost tender touch brushes
my fingertips. Later I wonder by what power—
was it the printed sign, demanding voice,
the child, my loneliness, my brave hand—
gave me that permission.

The Fisherman's Daughter

in a dream

In my father's outstretched hands,
a porgy, dark side bars, well above
the one-pound limit. *You shouldn't have
done it,* my child-voice says. On driftwood
he splays that porgy into an arch. Pins
the sharp spines into a still headdress.
Like a fisherman on a bamboo raft,
he dabs ink over flesh, freshly soaked,
stuffs paper under slits. Blood seeps
through protruding lips, as if, as if
to tell me the meaning of such gifts.
A father's gift is a daughter's catch.
Under a waxing gibbous moon,
I Q-tip the porgy's eye dry.

Photograph of an Oyster Dredge
Greenport Harbor (circa 1940)

On the Sailors Haven tour, we shake our heads looking
at a photo of oysters, piled as high as the wheelhouse windows,
distracting from the crane's teeth. The long-handled shovels
like Giacometti statues. The watermen's hulk.

Some watermen side-glance the camera eye. Some look down.
No longer feeling their hands? The photograph
is a secret about a secret. It's 1940.
The last year for oysters. Someone had a hunch.

Watermen. On the deck, rich
with industriousness, like ants carrying seeds
to their domed mounds. Scurrying
boats run out to sea. Farther, farther

down the line, we whisper
with the soft mouths of dreaming.
The oysters' mouths are shut,
like an oracle, speechless until spoken to.

Bucket to the Brim

to the Early Oyster Harvester

When the tide is low enough
the sea level below your knees,
you tug on rubber boots, thick-soled,
so no shards cut you. You
wade into gumbo mud,
with a hammer, ready to pry life off
the reef, Samson rope tied waist-high,
the bucket floats alongside you.
No license gives you sanction to rake
across the reef, with a heavy-toothed dredge
to harvest the smallest, sweetest meat
with slobber, lick, smack
lust-gush-gimme in murky waters—
Your bounty, off-season, forbidden.
No one sees the oyster thief.
When you fill your bucket,
may it spill.

Floods

Again, the causeway floods. Rings of rising
tides mark the raised road's stanchions,
the way you measure a child's height on a wall.

Behind a line of cars, my car. Water
deepening around the legs of the slickered
patrolman guiding our turnarounds.

I turn up the heater. Turn on talk radio.
A panel debates climate change—*Brr.*
So much for global warming, one man snickers.

The water's engine rolls out sheet after sheet. Sun
glances off the surface, so like the Delacroix painting
where light glances off a bedsheet,

where a man shows off his naked mistress
to her husband by holding a sheet in front of her face—
The husband shows no eyelash of recognition.

He doesn't see what he's lost,
the way we don't see how the rain
increases its sumptuous weeping. Now

I hear voices—the woman
in the painting and this flooded causeway saying:
Take a long look. I'm not going to be here forever.

Broken Free from Moorings

at Goldsmith's Beach, Southold, N.Y.

They ran toward me, the beach patrol,
cameras swinging, as I knelt next to the body—
a dead leatherback turtle lying on its back,
neck slit open, blood necklace,
like a jeweled choker. I was thinking—
This is the one with skin.
This is the one who sheds tears
as she lays eggs in a nest of sand.

Don't touch it, they kept saying.
Didn't they see my grimy fingers.
How could I touch the wound
of one who's swum in the sea's
dark cathedrals—

Get up, get up, they said,
because I was kneeling,
because I was in their camera shot.

I couldn't speak. It wasn't completely silent.
The buoys, those cords, they groaned,
that choke-back dug into the neck,
a continuous loop. In the Sound,

the mooring buoys tethered sail boats.
The buoys had been harmless when set,
saved sea pens of anemones from vessels beaching.

I had nowhere to go. When I stood,
the sand gave way underfoot.

Morning of The Great Whale Spirit

for Shane Weeks, Shinnecock Nation,
Shinnecock Nation's Ceremony
for the Great Whale, L.I., New York

The turtle-shell shaker in his hand,
its trembling ushers in chants,
rhythmic beats in the tongues of his Elders.
Low, guttural, half-sung words I don't know
but feel a prayer hum-quiver in my chest.
Dried sage burns in the abalone shell,
He crouches, shuffle-steps for the smoke cloud
to encircle the barely wet body, the body
Mother tide cannot reach. O hand,
O hand of the blessing work.
A life-hunting robot lands on Mars.
On the highway, electric cars motor along.
On this beach, he looks back
as if the smoke cleanses the space,
as if his father were calling his name,
or the sea calling to one of its own.

Theft

after the painting Dice Players *by Georges de la Tour (1650–1651)*

See the way light was stolen from Caravaggio.
Light-soaked, the dice roller's hand
in the "Come Here" position. The origin of candlelight
hidden but flooding men's faces. The dice table lit up

the way moonlight strobed a whale ship's deck. Imagine whalers
genuflecting when *rolling the bones*. The dice chiseled from
a whale's mouth bone. Each side of the dice, a carving of dots,
inked with tobacco juice—*alea iacta est*. Those dice.

If a man rolled a two, in the game of Hazard, he was out. Cheats
thrown overboard. After all, the plural of die is dice. Many prayed
to God for luck. Some assured His grace by drilling holes
in their personal dice, weighted each die with wax

from the live property of a whale's head. The wax hardened,
then melted when held in a cupped warm hand. *Mine,*
says the winning hand. No one sees light stolen
in a man's closed fist.

V.
*How to cipher where one life begins
and becomes another?*

—Linda Hull

Summer, Speaking in Turn

On the beach, a whale looks up at me
in blue crayon, drawn on a heart-shaped stone.
My finger traces the thick-lined body,
just as I did in my whale book at ten,
certain about their signs of happiness—
when flukes were held high,
just like the flukes on the stone I hold now.
It's July. High season for out-of-towners
when I face the bay only in early morning.
Why are you here? I ask the heart stone.
I don't know. Maybe the stone is a valentine
to be delivered by tidal whims to a whale
with a heart the size of a Harley. I pocket
the stone heart, the smile, the whale's face.

~

You've Got This—written with a red paint-pen
on a rock, then deliberately planted
on Race Point Beach by the artist.
Later that week, a woman will find the rock,
and in this loose communion, her smile
dolphins up. No longer is she a small raft,
a speck floating. She leaves
the rock in its sand bed hoping
children will discover it. Imagine
this kind of day when you don't expect to
find a friend. Yet you find one, featureless,
as alive as July. The beach is pulsing.

Ode to the Sea Turtle Rescuers

The high is what they are after:
to walk just after high tide.
When the drift line is glutted with kelp,
shells, lures, feathers, neon bits.
Shift walkers. They shamble up the shoreline,
falter and quick step to rescue footing
as they've done their whole lives. They trudge
forward with hope that their cell phone will stay
juiced beyond the dunes. They know
the phone number of the rescue truck.
They know luck: to find the tide's drop off spot.
They know the surrender of an empty beach,
the carapace of death. Cradling their own deaths,
they feel alive. Walking. In this world
with so many doses of decline at the foot
of the foredune, only this makes sense.
Walking. Only this.

Of Offerings

Where shoal grass meets sand, two chairs—green
plastic, high-backed—belonging to no one.
When I sit my spine recalls its wings,
a time when chairs could be wooden rafts
or lifeboats. I see my childhood bounding out
of the sea. No. It's a wild-haired, ginger dog.
A runaway. *Hello friend.* I tuck words into
the envelope of his ear. The dog
eats the lucky biscuit in my pocket.
I say, lucky, because I make my luck,
carry offerings to coax affection. *Good boy,* I say.
The dog's boy is soon beside us, panting
from his long run up the beach. *Odin.*
You'll never learn—he half-cries,
nuzzling the wet furry neck
looping his fingers under the dog's collar.
What is youth—all impulse to name a dog after a god,
to want god to sit beside us, so blood-close,
only to loosen our hold. I stare at the crest
of unbroken waves, the boy's unwavering gaze
on Odin's feathery tail, the beauty part, fanning joy.

Power Naps

They're motionless. Vertical. The mother sperm whale
napping with squid tentacles wilting from her mouth
like ribbons quivering in the current. Her calf sleeps,
tail standing too. They seem like carved shamans
between peace and precipice. How those muscled bodies
make me shiver, the large blunt heads almost comical,
the callosities shaped like archipelagos. Are they dreaming?
What is dream but clouds seeking abandoned shadows.
I dream about glass bottom boats, constellations, failing
Latin, falling, finding a secret room in my house.
Their spiracles are quiet. Do they dim the lights
in the brain room to stop breathing? I want answers.
But I can't find my body, to rise, to leave them.
How starstruck I am when a gold vein slips through
the crack of my unknowing, the futility of a sure thing—
when would the pencil drop from Einstein's hand
to wake him from a nap? There is no need for night.
Might Melville have written about a pale squid
if he'd seen this suspended grace? I read his mother
guarded her precious afternoon nap. The bliss
of slumber after repast, never belonging to mothers alone.

Scrolling Backward

The jitney travels to the long island
as this night recasts everything silky,
as the moon raises light on the landscape.

Scrolling backward, I recover that rust-spotted
ledger of lineage and hope, of *la mia famiglia,*
those women living in harbor towns,

where the night was a knife, where waves
trained your eyes on the one thing
you could see coming at you.

Who looks in a mirror to see what's behind
them? To think I've spent my life traversing
glass and frost, flame and loss,

those momentary tangos. And on the first day
living by the sea, to jump shallow waves
in the ways of the old women. My ancestor bones

leaping above this earth, drenched
in primal salt, returning to lightness,
cleansed into being.

Afterlife

Driftwood cast upon the sea's lashing,
slips through the fingers of waves,
colonized by gribbles, riddled with
pinholes from shipworms, hoppers,
wood piddocks, dressed in brine
at the wrack line—a woman
tosses driftwood into a pile of dunnage,
salvage bound for the old port dock.
On the dock, a man finds driftwood,
sunbaked, salt-smooth, the size of
a long-bone. Like Odin, he commands
the wood to *Cavort. Frolic. Frisk About.*
The man's lover strokes the wood's scars,
whorls, burled knots, deep striations in
chalk, wood ash, tinge of smoke,
singed quill feather gray. At her shop,
she twists lady orchids around the wood,
rhythms yellow petals into a dancing vine.
Drift, drift, drifting out of itself—I stare
in the shop window, my reflection shifts.
It's low tide. Waves fall and bloom what floats.
That sparkler. Earth's flint catching my breath.

Widening Rings

for Rachel Carson, Newcastle Inn, Southport, Maine

The wall photograph—taken right there—
of a girl, lying on her stomach, face almost touching
the tidal pond. Looking for what? Water fleas,
red-plumed tube worms, the widening rings of being.

How much time it takes to see—
as much time as it takes to make a friend—
cunners and hat pin urchins,
snails and gills, rock grit and us.

I've read about Aristotle and limpets,
how a muscled foot locomotes
into the sea to feed. How a limpet's shell
imprints like a scar/tattoo on the home-rock.

And the limpet always returns to the same spot.
Aristotle never figured out how
this homing works. A home can be
a room in an inn,

beyond the deep and wide Sheepscot,
sun-dried rocks glistening.

The Whale House

at Dead Man's Cove, Southold, NY

Autumn light slips off the corrugated roof
of the Whale House. No one there

except the broad skull, the jaw gape of a finback
whale strutted wall-to-wall, front to back.

I walk up to the sleek, bleached-out skele,
the hard envelope of its mouth. Never have I been as close

to sea's lightlessness. Gingerly placing my hand through
the window of the eye, bits of bone crumble onto my palm.

On a nearby shelf—this whale's baleen.
Bone-fringed bristles like hairbrushes

in the mouth. With one toothless gulp, the sea sieves out
the slurped-up small fry krill.

Such an immense body.
It would take a whole day to feel full.

I anchor the mouth bone to my lips. Blunt fumes,
the undigested fishiness fills my chest.

I am enormous. The sea floods into my open mouth—
its chills, fevers, shudders, bitters, the untranslatable whole of it,

the whole sea as swill and swallow. I drift below jagged swells
near the lighthouse. A green light sweeps over shipwrecked rocks.

Notes

"The End": The quote "Don't remember me, but ah! Remember my fate." is a restated line "Remember me! but Ah! forget my fate" from the aria "When I am laid in earth", in the opera *Dido and Aeneas* by Henry Purcell.

"Letter to Rachel Carson": In the introduction of *The Edge of the Sea,* Paul Brooks, Carson's friend and editor, said it was "significant that the text Rachel asked to be read at her funeral was from her writing about the sea." There is no mention of which friend promised to read Carson's desired passage.

"Photograph of an Oyster Dredge in Greenport Harbor, NY (1940)": The quote is from Diane Arbus: "The photograph is a secret about a secret. The more it tells you the less you know."

"Ishmael's Hands": was influenced by *A Whaler's Dictionary* by Dan Beachy-Quick.

Herman Melville's quote at the beginning of section 2 is from "Letter to Nathaniel Hawthorne, Monday Morning, 25th Oct: 1852" in the book *The Divine Magnet* edited by Mark Neimeyer.

"After Reading the Scrimshaw Dictionary, I Write Letters", "Letter to Joseph Bogart Hershey" and "Letter to Sereno Edward Bishop": was informed by *Scrimshaw and Provenance: The Third Dictionary of Scrimshaw Artists* by Stuart M. Frank, published by Mystic Seaport, Mystic, CT (2013).

"Missing": "According to marine biologists, the world's oldest known orca, thought to be over 100 years old, went missing in autumn 2016. They named her Granny, and tracked her for forty years as the matriarch for a large pod in the Salish Seas. . . where SeaWorld hunts for baby orcas for their Orlando theme park." Patrick Barkham, *The Guardian*.

"Ode to the Cold Stunned Sea Turtle": Every year, New York Marine Rescue Center asks volunteers to search for cold-stunned sea turtles stranded on Long Island's east end beaches. In 2023, volunteers found 95 cold stunned sea turtles, 48 survived. *New York Times,* "Where New York's Sick Sea Turtles Go For Rehab and Squid Snacks" by Dodai Stewart (February 24, 2023).

"Morning of the Great Whale Spirit": Details of this Shinnecock ceremony were viewed on L.I. Fox New York (Fox5NY.com) March 12, 2019; and on YouTube: *Shores of the Shinnecock—The Road Home* interview with Shane Weeks.

"Power Naps": after *Sea Legacy* co-founder and *National Geographic* contributor, Paul Nicklen's photograph entitled, "Suspended Grace."

About the Author

Vivian Eyre's poems have appeared in *The Bellingham Review, J Journal, One Art, Pangyrus, Quiddity, Spire, The Ashville Poetry Review, The Fourth River, The Massachusetts Review, The Orchards Journal,* and *Twelve Mile Journal.* Her ekphrastic poems inspired by Neo Rauch have appeared in the anthology, *Neu Smoke* (Off the Park Press). Eyre is the founder and facilitator since 2013 of a monthly poetry discussion series at Floyd Memorial Library in Greenport, New York, and is the moderator of a poetry conversation series at the Imago Foundation for the Arts in Warren, Rhode Island. In addition, she has served as guest curator for the Whale House at the Southold Historical Society Museum in Southold, New York, and as a cold-stunned sea turtle rescue volunteer for the New York Marine Rescue Center. Eyre lives with her standard poodle in Warren, RI.

www.ingramcontent.com/pod-product-compliance
Lightning Source LLC
Chambersburg PA
CBHW030911170426
43193CB00009BA/807